GOD'S
HEART
FOR THE
NATIONS

JEFF LEWIS

ISBN: 9780989954525

To order another copy of this Bible study, visit *Pioneers.org/Store*. All people group profiles were provided by Pioneers.

To inquire regarding content, contact Jeff Lewis, c/o California Baptist University, 8432 Magnolia Avenue, Riverside, CA 92504-3297. E-mail: lewis_jc@msn.com.

Scripture quotations are from The Holy Bible, English Standard Version® (ESV®), copyright © 2001 by Crossway, a publishing ministry of Good News Publishers. Used by permission. All rights reserved.

All missionary quotes were taken from the book, World Shapers, compiled by Vinita Hampton and Carol Plueddemann, Harold Shaw Publishing, Wheaton, Illinois.

Design and layout by Joe DeLeon.

If I were asked to choose one verse to summarize the essence of the Bible, it would be Psalm 46:10. Many Christians know the first part but don't realize there is more to the verse. We love the personal benefits of, "Be still, and know that I am God," but we consciously or unconsciously disconnect that from its global implications, and develop an evangelical theology that places man at the center and neglects God's purpose in the world.

The major focus of American Christian thought and practice may seem to be "What can God do for me?" Our lives reflect a belief that God's global priority is to make His disciples more comfortable. Don't get me wrong, I believe that God desires to bless us and that God's desire to bless His people is a major theme of the Bible. But if we focus on the theme of blessing alone, we distort the truth and lose the context in which God's blessings are given.

The purpose of this study is to help create an awareness of one of the most ignored themes of the Bible – God's global purpose: His desire and activity of redeeming mankind, the nations, to Himself. It involves the active pursuit of worshipers from all the peoples of the earth that will give Him the glory due His name. God's blessings and His global purpose are beautifully woven together in the Bible. My conviction is that in order to correctly interpret and apply scripture, it is essential to understand the connection of these two themes. To ignore either one leads to misinterpretation and faulty application. Ultimately, lives will be misdirected.

I pray that the Holy Spirit will open your eyes to the truth of His Word as you progress through this study, and that you will respond to His guidance in applying His truth.

Jeff Lewis

lewis_jc@msn.com

INTRODUCTION

Video Introduction
by Jeff Lewis
pioneers.org/godsheart

BEFORE YOU GET STARTED

There are a few things that you need to know in order to get the most from this study. I have deliberately added little commentary to each lesson. This is not because I couldn't think of anything to say. My personal tendency is to say too much, but you have a Teacher who will guide you in all the truth.

❶ **The Holy Spirit will teach and lead you in the truth.**

"But the Helper, the Holy Spirit, whom the Father will send in My name, He will teach you all things and bring to your remembrance all that I have said to you" (John 14:26).

"When the Spirit of truth comes, He will guide you into all the truth..." (John 16:13).

"These things God has revealed to us through the Spirit. For the Spirit searches everything, even the depths of God. For who knows a person's thoughts except the spirit of that person, which is in him? So also no one comprehends the thoughts of God except the Spirit of God. Now we have received not the spirit of the world, but the Spirit who is from God, that we might understand the things freely given us by God. And we impart this in words not taught by human wisdom but taught by the Spirit, interpreting spiritual truths to those who are spiritual" (1 Corinthians 2:10-13).

Every time you come into contact with God's Word through study, reading, hearing, memorizing, and meditation, ask the Holy Spirit to give you wisdom and understanding. As you interact with the Word of God, be faithfully interacting with the Spirit of God.

❷ **The word of God is living, powerful, and transforming.**

"Is not My Word like fire, declares the LORD, and like a hammer that breaks the rock in pieces?" (Jeremiah 23:29)

"All Scripture is breathed out by God and profitable for teaching, for reproof, for correction, and for training in righteousness, that the man of God may be complete, equipped for every good work" (2 Timothy 3:16-17).

"For the Word of God is living and active, sharper than any two-edged sword, piercing to the division of soul and of spirit, of joints and of marrow, and discerning the thoughts and intentions of the heart" (Hebrews 4:12).

Too often I approach my time in God's Word as a duty that I mindlessly plod through. I walk through the corridors of the Bible like a self-absorbed teenager walking through a mall. I need to be reminded of the words of Proverbs 2:1-5:

*"My son, if you receive my words
and treasure up my commandments with you,
making your ear attentive to wisdom*

and inclining your heart to understanding;
yes, if you call out for insight
and raise your voice for understanding
if you seek it like silver
and search for it as for hidden treasures,
Then you will understand the fear of the LORD
and find the knowledge of God."

Don't rush through this study or any other time you interact with His Word. Come and drink deeply from the revelation of His mind and pull up your chair to feed from the lavish banquet table of His Word.

"Your words were found, and I ate them,
and your words became to me a joy
and the delight of my heart,
for I am called by your name,
O LORD, God of hosts" (Jeremiah 15:16).

❸ **Memorization and meditation will advance you beyond interpreting the Bible through your biases and filter of need.**

During your journey through this study you will have the opportunity to fix your attention on specific aspects of scriptural truth. Faithful memorization and meditation on God's Word will play a key role in the discovery process.

In each lesson I have selected a passage to memorize which captures a key element in the study. For consistency, all scriptures quoted in this booklet are in the ESV version. You are, however, encouraged to use the translation of your choice both for the study and the memorization. As you memorize and meditate on a verse, the Holy Spirit will begin to turn His floodlight of illumination and understanding on the meaning. My prayer is that God would "open your eyes, that you may behold wondrous things out of His law." (Psalm 119:18).

Many of us haven't memorized scripture since we were children (if then), but it is not as hard as it may seem.

1. Start with the reference: the book, chapter, and verse(s).

2. Then add the first phrase of the verse, and say the reference again.

3. Each time you say the passage, add one more phrase. Start and end with the reference each time so you will remember it and bring the verse to mind whenever you see or hear the reference.

4. Many also find it helpful to copy the verse out by hand and put it someplace they will see it regularly throughout the week.

What is meditation? John Piper defines meditation as follows:

"The word 'meditation' in Hebrew means basically to speak or to mutter. When this is done in the heart it is called musing or meditation. So meditating on the Word of God day and night means to speak to yourself the Word of God day and night and to speak to yourself about it."

I would describe my personal practice of meditation as a prayerful conversation with God about His Word. I come with wonder, questions, issues, and longing to understand and obey.

As you are memorizing the selected scripture for each lesson, I would ask that you commit to the following:

1. Choose a phrase or verse to focus on for the day.

2. Select specific times throughout the day for brief meditation retreats of about 3-5 minutes each. Choose times during natural daily transitions; before meals, between classes, during break times, etc. Until it becomes a natural movement of your life, you could also set alerts on your phone remind you.

3. Ponder each word or phrase of the text and prayerfully capture as many insights as you can. Visualize the text and concepts in your mind.

4. Picture sitting at the feet of Christ and having the opportunity to talk with Him about His Word. As God begins to illuminate His truth to your heart and mind, begin to pray the scripture back to God.

5. No matter how your day has gone, choose to meditate on the text as you lay down for the night.

All this takes time. It means we have to slow down. By now you should understand that it will be difficult to get the most out of this study if you do it quickly.

❹ The role of the fellowship/church

You may work through this study with a group or on your own, but even if you are studying by yourself, please remember that the Christian life is not a solo act. Share what you are learning with others who are part of your fellowship. They may be able to correct or provide balance for any questionable interpretations or faulty conclusions.

Fellow followers of Christ may also be intrigued or challenged by what you learn, and want to join your journey of discovery. "Therefore encourage one another and build one another up, just as you are doing" (1 Thessalonians 5:11). The Greek word for "encourage" carries with it the idea of exhortation, comfort, and instruction and "build up" speaks of promoting growth in Christian wisdom and devotion. To live this out, don't keep what God shows you to yourself.

❺ Format – basic elements to the study

A. **Memory Verses –** I have selected a passage each week that communicates the very essence of that week's study. Don't blow it off or just memorize it to fulfill your duty. Treasure God's Word in your heart and prepare yourself to be blown away by the illuminated insights that only the Holy Spirit can reveal.

B. **Bible Passages –** Read the verses listed. Take your time and read through the verses a few times. Read them in the context of a conversation with God. When appropriate, personalize the verse. Take the time to write out your response in the space provided.

C. **Comments and Questions –** These are meant to guide you in the discovery process. The questions will be used to provoke response or create more questions. I have no illusions that this study will satisfy all your questions. My prayer is that it will create more questions and motivate you to develop an investigative lifestyle in relation to God's Word.

D. Quotations – I have included quotations from the "great cloud of witnesses" that have gone before us. Brothers and sisters in the faith who have lived for the glory of God and responded to His global call speak from the nucleus of their journey of obedience. The words they spoke reflected their passion for God and His purpose that forged the world for God's glory. Interacting with their words is your brief opportunity to walk with them.

E. Prayer Focus – Each week you will be given information about an unreached population or people group. Throughout the week you are to become an intercessor before the throne of grace on their behalf.

F. Pauses – Have you noticed the word *Selah* when reading through the Psalms? *Selah* is a technical musical term meaning accentuation and pause. As you read, take the psalmist's advice and pause to reflect and meditate on what God is communicating through His Word. Watch for the word *Selah* through the study; it will be used to remind you to pause.

The term will also be used to indicate the natural pauses in each lesson. You can complete each study in one sitting or extend your study throughout the week. I recommend that you not hurry, but use the natural pauses to remind yourself of the need to stay spiritually and mentally engaged with the Word.

SELAH

WHERE TO FIND THE PEOPLE GROUPS

(WITH PAGE REFERENCES)

◄ THE FRENCH *(P.45)*

◄ PEOPLES OF THE NORTH CAUCASUS *(P.39)*

PUNJABI SIKHS *(P.51)* ►

RAJPUTS OF INDIA *(P.33)* ►

◄ PEOPLES OF CHAD *(P.14)*

◄ PEOPLES OF MYANMAR *(P.21)*

◄ SOUTHEAST ASIAN MUSLIMS *(P.27)*

Video Introduction
by Jeff Lewis
pioneers.org/godsheart

FOR THE GLORY OF GOD

Ⓜ To Memorize and Meditate On

Oh sing to the LORD a new song;
* sing to the LORD, all the earth!*
Sing to the LORD, bless His name;
* tell of His salvation from day to day.*
Declare His glory among the nations,
* His marvelous works among all the peoples!*

— Psalm 96:1-3

"With Thee, O my God, is no disappointment. I shall never have to regret that I have loved Thee too well."

— Henry Martyn, British missionary to India and Persia

GETTING STARTED

Why did God create the heavens and the earth? Why did God create men and women? What is the chief aim of God? Not His only passion or motivation, but His ultimate passion for which all other passions are subordinate. When every other reason is eliminated but one, what remains? This would be His ultimate design of creation.

In the early years of my walk with Jesus Christ, I lived under the illusion that Christianity was about me. I thought that I (man) was the center of God's world; that my needs were the basis for His actions. I believed that the ultimate purpose of God was to grant me salvation and enjoy me forever. This perspective naturally led me to believe that the ultimate objective of missions was man.

As you study this lesson, I challenge you to not bring your template of understanding to the Bible, but look afresh with the knowledge that the Holy Spirit will grant you. As you read the following verses, reflect on these questions: What does the Bible say is the ultimate goal of God? What is the ultimate purpose of His activity in the world?

❶ The God Who Delivers

Of all the events of the Bible, God's deliverance of Israel from their Egyptian capturers would seem to be rooted in God's responding to the desperate need of His people (Exodus 3:9). But Ezekiel 20:5-14 and other passage put the event in a larger context.

a. What was God's offer to Israel? (Ezekiel 20:6)

b. What was their response to His offer? (Ezekiel 20:8)

c. Why does God say He acted this way? (Ezekiel 20:9, 14)

d. Why did God deliver Israel from captivity? (2 Samuel 7:22-23)

e. As the Egyptian chariots were attacking the Israelites trapped by the Red Sea, what was the people's reaction? (Psalm 106:7-12)

f. Why did God rescue them? (Psalm 106:8; Isaiah 63:12-14)

❷ For the Sake of His Name

Read the following passages and record what God does for the "sake of His name."

a. Isaiah 43:25; 1 John 2:12

b. Psalm 143:11

c. Psalm 31:3

d. Daniel 9:17-19

e. Philippians 1:29

God is jealous for His name and for His glory. We were created to be the image bearers of God, to reflect and manifest His glory in the world (Genesis 1:26-28; Isaiah 43:7). I used to treat phrases like "for the glory of God" as religious tack-on phrases. Phrases like this are not to give emphasis to the main point – they are the main point.

SELAH

❸ To the Glory of God the Father

Record how Jesus' life, death, resurrection, and ascension relate to the glory of God.

a. John 13:31-32; 17:4

b. John 12:27-28

c. Romans 6:4

d. Philippians 2:9-11

❹ Do It All for the Glory of God

Notice some of the different ways that followers of Jesus Christ are called to glorify God.

a. 1 Corinthians 6:20, 10:31

b. 1 Peter 4:11

c. 1 Peter 4:16

d. John 21:18-19

e. Psalm 72:19, 86:9; Habakkuk 2:14

f. Matthew 5:13-16

GLORY. Throughout the ages books have been written to declare the meaning of this word. It seems so transcendent to me that I cower from trying to understand it. Consider the following: It is the splendor, majesty, honor, and reputation of God. Glory is used to describe the power of God. The Hebrew word most often translated "glory" in the Old Testament is *kabad*, which means to be heavy, weighty, or honored. God's glory is the weightiness of the presence of the holy and majestic God. God's glory is the manifestation of God's character, attributes, and actions as He invades human reality. On another level, the term speaks of our delight, boasting, and praise of God. We glorify God as God manifests Himself in us through our words and actions. We glorify God as we recognize Him in our obedience, confession, praise, delight, and service in the world.

God's passion for His name and His glory is the supreme reason for His actions in the world. This does not lessen the fact that He loves us; in fact, it strengthens the concept of His love for us. This Bible study is built on this foundational truth. God's passion for His name should be our central motivation for world evangelization. God is not receiving the worship that is due His name; therefore, the mission of the Church is to call out worshippers from among the nations. Every church and every follower of Jesus Christ is called to participate in this global activity.

As pastor and author John Piper puts it in his book *Let the Nations Be Glad*, "God is pursuing with omnipotent passion a worldwide purpose of gathering joyful worshippers for Himself from every tribe and tongue and people and nation. He has an inexhaustible enthusiasm for the supremacy of His name among the nations. Therefore, let us bring our affections into line with His, and for the sake of His name, let us renounce the quest for worldly comforts and join His global purpose."

❼ Meditation

a. Stop and reflect on what God is teaching you.

b. Begin a habit of praying for unreached peoples by reading the profile at the end of each lesson (meet the peoples of Chad on page 14 for this lesson).

"The presence of God became unutterably real and blessed, and I remember ... stretching myself on the ground and lying there before him with unspeakable awe and unspeakable joy. For what service I was accepted I knew not, but a deep consciousness that I was not my own took possession of me which has never since been effaced."

— J. Hudson Taylor

SELAH

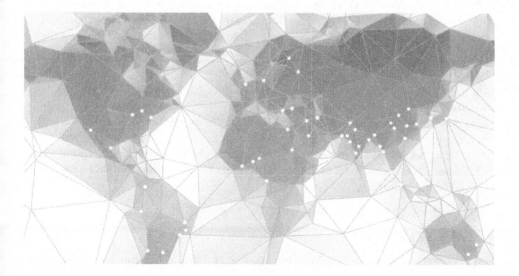

PEOPLES OF CHAD

W e live in one of the least-reached places of Africa, on the edge of the Sahara," explains Dave, leader of a mission team. "It's a three-day drive from the capital. In our town there are no paved roads, no electricity, and no running water. We live on the edge."

Other places may be easier to get to, but often times it's the forgotten places like this that haven't been touched with God's Word. Half of Chad's 140 people groups are still considered unreached by the gospel. That makes the country home to more unreached groups than any other African country.

Like some of its neighbors, Chad has historically been divided between Arab-influenced Muslims in the north and black African Christians and animists in the south.

Muslims are in the majority. People with whom Dave works have been Muslims for hundreds of years and are surrounded by other groups that are also Muslim. They find it difficult to even consider any alternative.

Chad is surprisingly open to Christian witness, however, and some Muslims are spiritually hungry and responsive to the gospel. The Bible storytelling efforts of local and foreign Christians are starting to bear fruit as many hear the gospel for the first time. And hearing does seem to be the key. A high percentage of Chadians are not literate, and many are better able to grasp and pass on what they hear better than what they might read.

Opportunities to help meet physical needs are also abundant. Health care, access to clean water, and community development projects are desperately needed. Chad is one of the poorest countries in the world. It regularly ranks high on lists of the most corrupt countries.

The physical challenges and stresses of life on the edge can be overwhelming for those who serve here. Ministry itself can be discouraging. "Spiritual warfare is real here," says Dave. "There is a definite sense that Satan does not want the Word to be sown here. People are generally open to talking about religion, but life change is much harder to come by."

In the capital, *N'Djamena* (ehn-jah-MAY-nah), things are a little different. More than a million people live in and around Chad's only city and include representatives from each corner of the country. The city is also home to thousands of Christians of various backgrounds. Some meet in ethnic churches and others in French-speaking multi-ethnic churches. We can pray for the growth, unity, and effectiveness of the Christians in N'Djamena and other parts of the country and that some of them would be called to reach out cross-culturally.

❶ **Prayer Points**

- Pray for the Church to be stirred and equipped for evangelism among an increasing Muslim majority. (Acts 4:29-30)

- Pray for pioneer missionaries to persevere in difficult places in order to reach the unreached. (2 Corinthians 4:7)

- Pray for integrity and honesty to rule the nation and displace government corruption. (1 Timothy 2:1-4)

❷ Go Deeper

- Watch a Pioneers video about Dave's team and their life and ministry in Chad at *vimeo.com/34524104.*

- Learn more from *prayercast.com/chad* and *operationworld.org/chad.*

LESSON TWO

GOD'S BLESSING AND PURPOSE

Ⓜ **To Memorize and Meditate On**

Now the LORD said to Abram, "Go from your country and your kindred and your father's house to the land that I will show you. And I will make of you a great nation, and I will bless you and make your name great, so that you will be a blessing. I will bless those who bless you, and him who dishonors you I will curse, and in you all the families of the earth shall be blessed."

— Genesis 12:1-3

"While vast continents are shrouded in darkness ... the burden of proof lies upon you to show that the circumstances in which God has placed you were meant by God to keep you out of the foreign mission field."

—Ion Keith-Faloner, Scottish missionary and Arabic scholar

GETTING STARTED

In this study we will approach the Bible not as 66 books that happen to be bound by one cover, but as one book. The Bible has an introduction, a body, and a conclusion. The introduction is the first eleven chapters of Genesis, the body starts with Genesis chapter 12 and runs through Jude, and the conclusion is Revelation.

An author will begin to surface major themes in the introduction. One of the keys to the correct interpretation of the Bible is to detect these themes and track how the author develops them throughout the book. It is foolish to try to interpret the Bible without some idea of its emphasis and purpose. This lesson looks at two basic themes which first appear in Genesis 1:28.

"And God blessed them. And God said to them, "Be fruitful and multiply and fill the earth and subdue it, and have dominion over the fish of the sea and over the birds of the heavens and over every living thing that moves on the earth."

The first theme is that God desires to bless His creation. In the context of blessing we discover the second theme, dealing with God's purpose and man's responsibility. The two themes are restated in Genesis 9:1 and further defined in Genesis 12:1-3. Before we look at Genesis 12 in greater depth, let's summarize what happens in the introduction of the Bible.

1. God has created the heavens and the earth and all living things, the crown of His creation being Adam and Eve. They sinned and destroyed their relationship with God; God pursued them, judged them and the serpent, and He sacrificed animals,

revealing that the shedding of blood is necessary for the covering of sin.

2. Man continues to multiply but in so doing continued in his rebellion against God to the point that man's sin was so grievous that God had to judge mankind with a flood. We continue to see God's redemptive character revealed in delivering Noah's family from the flood.

3. The generations after Noah continued to reject God's authority. In the land of Shinar the people sought to make a name for themselves by building a city and a tower whose top reached to the heavens, in order not to be "dispersed over the face of the whole earth" (Genesis 11:4), though this was an act of disobedience to God's first command to fill and subdue the earth.

4. With a catastrophic judgment, God confused their language and "dispersed them from there over the face of all the earth" (Genesis 11:8). The result of God's judgment was the creation of approximately 70 distinct family groups listed in Genesis 10.

This is the backdrop from which God calls Abram to leave his country and declares His covenant to him.

❶ The Covenant with Abram

Read Genesis 12:1-3. List the three ways God said He would bless Abraham.

a.

b.

c.

What do verses 2 and 3 tell us about God's purposes in this covenant?

a.

b.

Notice that the two statements about purpose reveal why God has chosen to bless Abram and give further definition to the theme of purpose/responsibility.

a. Why has God blessed Abram?

b. Who are the families to which Abram is to be a blessing? (See Genesis 11:1-9)

c. Read Galatians 3:7-9, and see how Paul explains Genesis 12:3. How does this help you define what the gospel of Christ is?

❷ A Covenant for All Peoples

a. In Genesis 17:1-8 we see God change Abram's name to Abraham. The name Abram means "exalted father." What does Abraham mean? (See 17:5.)

b. In Genesis 12:2, what had God promised Abraham in relation to a nation?

c. What does God promise Abraham in Genesis 17:5-6?

d. As God continues to define His covenant with Abraham, we discover His redemptive mission that people from all nations and peoples will become children of Abraham. How does Paul interpret this declaration of the covenant? (See Romans 4:16-17 and Galatians 3:29.)

❸ Restating the Covenant

God later confirmed His covenant with Abraham and repeats it to Isaac and Jacob, clarifying the themes. Read the following verses and write down your reflections. Notice the analogies used to communicate Israel's role in God's global purpose.

a. Genesis 22:16-18

b. Genesis 26:3-5

c. Genesis 28:14

As we journey through the Bible we will discover the parallel nature of the two themes of blessing and God's purpose/man's responsibility. The pitfall is failing to keep these two themes in their parallel tension. Our tendency is to see God's blessings disconnected from His purpose. That perspective will create an egocentric faith.

❹ **More Narratives of Blessing and Purpose**

Consider what God was doing in each of these Old Testament stories. You can either answer these questions reflecting on what you've been taught in the past or with what we've learned from the first two lessons. We'll look more closely at these questions in the next lesson.

a. Why did God part the Red Sea?

b. Why did God give Solomon wisdom?

c. Why did God give Israel His commandments?

d. Why did God deliver Daniel from the lion's den?

e. Finish the following verse from memory. "Be still …"

Reflect on your answers and determine to which of the two themes your answers relate. Put a "B" next to the answers that relate to the theme of blessing and a "P" next to the answers that relate to God's purpose. To which theme did your answers most relate?

❺ **Meditation**

a. Write down what God has been teaching you through meditation on Genesis 12:1-3.

b. Summarize what you have learned from this lesson.

c. Pray for the nations using the people group profile on the next page.

"I have seen, at different times, the smoke of a thousand villages - villages whose people are without Christ, without God, and without hope in the world."

— Robert Moffat

S E L A H

PRAYER PROFILE

PEOPLES OF MYANMAR

Myanmar (mee-YAHN-mahr), or Burma, is home to more than 52 million people in some 135 ethnic groups, most of them unreached by the gospel. Though the country is rich in resources, its people have suffered under decades of military dictatorship. Many, especially minorities, still live in desperate poverty.

But today things are changing. Myanmar is opening up and becoming more democratic as well as more developed, bringing the people opportunity to improve their lives. And more are able to learn about finding new life in Jesus Christ, even when that means leaving Buddhism, Islam, and other faiths of their forefathers.

It seems that all over the world – even in Myanmar – are those God is giving a holy discontent, a restlessness that motivates them to seek after him. Ko Kan (KOH KAHN) is just such a person.

"I was without hope in my life… I felt my life had no meaning, so I became a Buddhist monk," the young man explains. "I strove, labored, and was very diligent. I became exalted among the Buddhist people around me. However, within me was emptiness. I was incomplete. So I went into the jungle to practice Buddhism by myself. I thought, 'If I keep striving, I might just achieve Nirvana (nuhr-VAH-nah, perfect peace).'"

Fasting and following Buddhist practices, Ko Kan became so weak from hunger that he fainted. "I came to see that these practices could only end in death for me. So I left that life and continued my search."

"It's very amazing how God redeemed me. It says in Genesis that this world was empty, formless, and dark. And just like when God said, 'Let there be light,' a friend came from America and taught me the Bible for four years. It was then that I experienced the love of God."

"He came to faith in Christ," says Ko Kan's American friend. "He came to see the many teachers he'd had in his life had wanted to take advantage of him but that Christ wanted to give Himself for Ko Kan, that Christ gave Himself for His disciples. That was different than any other teacher that he had seen or even heard of. It really impressed him."

While most of Myanmar's believers come from a few minority groups, members of the Buddhist majority, including monks like Ko Kan, are now responding. As an indigenous mission movement begins to flourish, momentum for continued evangelism is building.

❶ **Prayer Points**

- Ask God to raise up and equip more laborers willing to live and serve in a difficult place like Myanmar. (Matthew 9:35-38)
- Pray for fruitful collaboration between foreign Christian missionaries and

national believers as they work together to reach the nation for Christ. (Psalm 133)

- Lift up efforts to translate the scriptures into the many languages of the peoples of Myanmar, that everyone may receive the Word of God in the language of their hearts. (Hebrews 4:12)

❷ **Go Deeper**

- Watch Pioneers videos about Myanmar at *commnetmedia.com*. Follow political events and other news at *burmanet.org/news*. Join Christians concerned for this nation through *prayforburma.org*.

- See also *operationworld.org/myan* and watch the Prayercast video at *prayercast.com/myanmar*.

LESSON THREE

GOD IMPACTS THE NATIONS AS HE BLESSES HIS PEOPLE

Ⓜ To Memorize and Meditate On

*"Be still, and know that I am God.
I will be exalted among the nations,
I will be exalted in the earth!"*

— Psalm 46:10

"How often do we attempt work for God to the limit of our incompetency rather than to the limit of God's omnipotency."

— J. Hudson Taylor, missionary to China

GETTING STARTED

In this lesson you will study portions of the Bible that reveal how the two themes of God's blessing and His purpose interface. As God blessed the people of Israel He would reveal Himself to the nations and draw Gentiles to Himself.

❶ Revisiting Familiar Stories

While working through the following passages, pay attention to how both themes are woven together in Bible stories that you may know well. Notice how God's blessings are used to impact the nations and how individuals respond. Also, take some time to reflect on why you think the second theme of God's purpose and man's responsibility is usually ignored when these stories are discussed. Make note of your observations.

a. God's judgment of Egypt with ten plagues (Exodus 5:1-2; 7:5, 17; 8:10, 19; 9:13-17, 29)

b. The parting of the Red Sea (Joshua 4:23-24, 2:8-11)

c. The commands and statutes that God gave Israel (Deuteronomy 4:5-8)

d. God blessing Solomon with wisdom (1 Kings 4:29-34, 10:1-9)

e. God delivering Daniel from the lions' den (Daniel 6:16-28)

f. God blessing Esther and Mordecai (Esther 8:15-18)

❷ **Write Out Psalm 46:10**

S E L A H

❸ **Understanding God's Global Purpose**

One question that needs to be asked is whether any of the Old Testament characters understood both of these themes. Did their actions or prayers reveal their understanding of the connection between God's desire to bless His people and His purpose of declaring Himself to the nations? Did they understand their responsibility in God's global purpose? In the following verses, is there anything that would indicate to you that these men understood the two themes that we are studying?

a. Abraham interceding for Sodom (Genesis 18:16-33)

1. Why does the Lord consider telling Abraham what He is about to do? (16-19)

2. Which themes are mentioned?

3. What is Abraham's response to the Lord's announcement of His pending judgment on Sodom and Gomorrah?

4. Abraham's response indicates his understanding of what theme?

b. Moses interceding for Israel (Numbers 14:11-19)

1. The first part of his prayer relates to what theme? (13-16)

2. In your own words, express what Moses is saying in the first part of his intercession.

3. On what theme is the second part of Moses' prayer based? (17-19)

c. David's song of thanks (1 Chronicles 16:7-36). David proclaims a psalm of thanksgiving after the Ark of the Covenant is returned to the city of David. Throughout this psalm David reveals his understanding of God's global purpose. Record the five verses that indicate David's understanding of this theme.

1.

2.

3.

4.

5.

d. Solomon's dedication of the temple (1 Kings 8:22-43). After the temple had been completed, Solomon prays a prayer of dedication. Find the portion of the prayer that indicates Solomon's understanding of God's global purpose and explain what Solomon is asking.

❹ Meditation

a. Take some time to reflect on what you have discovered in the verses you have studied this week. What has the Holy Spirit revealed to you? Write those insights down and consider how you might apply them in your daily walk with Jesus Christ. Include any insights from your meditation on Psalm 46:10.

b. Pray for the nations using the people group profile for this lesson.

"If I had not felt certain that every additional trial was ordered by infinite love and mercy, I could not have survived my accumulated sufferings."

— Adoniram Judson, American missionary to Burma

SELAH

SOUTHEAST ASIAN MUSLIMS

It's 4:30 am in Pontianak (pohnt-ee-AH-nakh), Indonesia, and the call to prayer echoes out over the otherwise quiet city. Adin (ah-DEEN) is already awake and has washed his head, face, hands, and feet. He walks to the mosque a few steps from his apartment. A life-long friend, less devout, just rolls over in bed. His boathouse on the river is docked in front of a local mosque, but the voice on the loud speaker is not enough to rouse him. Both men are Malay (mah-LAY), though, and to be Malay is to be Muslim.

More than 225 million Muslims, some 20 percent of Muslims worldwide, call Southeast Asia home. Many live in Malaysia and Indonesia, from villages along the riverbanks and tropical rain forests to the high-rises and slums of mega-cities like Kuala Lumpur and Jakarta. Others can be found in Singapore and Brunei, or live among the Buddhists and Christians of Thailand, the Philippines, and Myanmar.

The Malay and other Indo-Malay peoples feel Islam is what keeps their cultures rooted in the midst of a changing world. Theirs is a gentler face of Islam than you might see in some places; after being Muslim, they consider being kind and friendly the signs of a good person. They take particular care to preserve peace and harmony, offer hospitality, behave respectably, and avoid conflict and debate. They may also be reticent to speak about personal problems lest they cause others to worry.

Southeast Asian Muslims have a strong awareness of the spiritual world and work to avoid or appease *jinn* (evil spirits). They may fear being left alone or encountering spirits in dark places. Like his friends and neighbors, Adin has experience with ghosts, spirits, and those who have been possessed or harassed by them. Many will turn to a traditional healer, often called a *dukun* (doo-KOON) for protection, and look to religious devotion to keep evil at bay and earn them blessings.

Seeking safety and security, some Southeast Asian communities see the appeal of *sharia* (shah-REE-ah, or Islamic law), and politicians appeal to others by promising more Islamic laws in exchange for votes.

❶ **Prayer Points**

- Lift up the hearts of Southeast Asians struggling to preserve safety and harmony in a changing and sometimes dangerous world. May they call out to the God who can deliver them. (Isaiah 61:1)

- Some Southeast Asian groups have growing Christian populations. Thank God for those who are reaching out to their neighbors, and pray that more would respond to this call. (Romans 10:14-15)

- Pray for spiritual breakthrough among the diverse Southeast Asian Muslim people groups. May hearts be prepared for the message. (John 6:44)

 Go Deeper

- Watch a Pioneers video about what church-planting ministry in this region may look like at *vimeo.com/29370879*. Get a snapshot of Indonesia at *operationworld.org/indo*.

- To learn more about the many Southeast Asian Muslim groups, how they differ from one another, and how to pray for them go to *apeopleloved.com*.

LESSON FOUR

THE PSALMS AND PROPHETS REVEAL GOD'S HEART FOR THE NATIONS

Ⓜ To Memorize and Meditate On

*May God be gracious to us and bless us
and make His face to shine upon us, Selah
that Your way may be known on earth,
Your saving power among all nations.
Let the peoples praise You, O God;
let all the peoples praise You!*

— *Psalm 67:1-3*

"He is no fool who gives what he cannot keep to gain what he cannot lose." — Jim Elliot

GETTING STARTED

We do not worship a tribal deity or the god of a region, a people, or a country. We worship the God of all nations. This truth is reflected in the psalms of Israel. Psalms reveals God's heart for the nations, God's call for the nations to worship Him, and the declaration of praise among the nations by His people.

❶ Ruler of the Nations

Take your time and meditate on the following psalms and write down your reflections. Note that when the psalmists use the word "peoples," they are referring to the nations. Consider the following questions:

- What is God telling the nations to do?

- What is God telling us to do among the nations?

- What is God saying to the nations?

a. Psalm 2:1-12

b. Psalm 22:25-31

c. Psalm 57:7-11

d. Psalm 66:1-8

e. Psalm 72:8-20

f. Psalm 96:1-13

g. Psalm 98:1-9

SELAH

---

❷ Prophet to the Nations

The prophets were continually proclaiming God's desire to be known, worshiped, and served by the nations. They also revealed the future fulfillment of the nations coming to God. You know the drill… now go dig for treasures.

a. What does Isaiah 19:18-25 teach will happen to the enemies of Israel?

b. What does Isaiah 42:6-13 say the light of the nations will accomplish?

c. Take a look at Jeremiah's calling (Jeremiah 1:5) and one of his proclamations (16:19-21). What do you notice?

d. What does Ezekiel 36:16-23 say is God's motivation for scattering and restoring Israel?

e. Why does Daniel 7:13-14 say the "son of man" was presented to the "Ancient of Days"?

f. What does Micah 4:1-5 say will happen when the nations come to the mountain of the Lord?

g. In Malachi 1:11, what does God declare about His name?

---

❸ Israel's Response, Our Response

The four lessons that you have completed are in no way exhaustive of Old Testament passages that connect with God's global purpose. Pause for a moment.

b. Why do you think that most of Israel seemed to miss the connection between God's blessings and His purpose and their responsibility in that purpose?

c. Have we missed it? If your answer is yes, why do you think we have missed it?

Father, release me from the slavery of an egocentric faith. Awaken me to the reality that Christ's death on the cross delivered me from the slavery of living for myself. (See 2 Corinthians 5:15.)

SELAH

❹ Meditation

a. What has God been teaching you from Psalm 67? Take some time and consider how God has blessed you. How have you connected His blessings with His desire to reach the nations?

b. Pray for the nations using the people group profile on the next page.

In the next lesson you will begin to study the New Testament, where the focus will be on how the themes of blessing and purpose are defined in the person of Jesus Christ. He is the incomparable blessing promised to Abram and his children (Israel) and through them to the nations. Through His life, ministry, and teachings, Jesus also clarifies for us God's global purpose.

"Proclaim the Word more and argue about it less."
— William Cameron Townsend, pioneer of Bible translation

S E L A H

PRAYER PROFILE

RAJPUTS OF INDIA

The Rajput (RAHJ-puht) people are descendents of the *maharajas* who once ruled North India. When India gained its independence from Britain in 1947 and formed a democratic government, they found themselves suddenly lacking means of financial support and were forced to sell their possessions or convert their palaces into hotels. Today some live a life of privilege and prosperity, while others struggle to get by.

Rajputs worship a myriad of gods and goddesses, visit temples, and give offerings. Some read Hindu scriptures, and many heed the advice of astrologers. Lata (LAH-tah), aged 20 and very devout, prays daily in the *puja* (POO-jah, worship) room of her home where a shelf with small figurines of the gods helps her focus. "I don't want to be evil or to be reincarnated. I worry about that happening. In the last life, I must have done only a few things bad, so the gods have given me another chance as a human being. Since they have, I want to continue my *pujas* and do good deeds so eventually I will go on to heaven."

Madhu (mah-DOO) worships for a different reason. "For the last six years I have been under the sign of the sun and it has been ruling me. If I don't worship the sun in the morning, it will bring bad things into my life."

In today's India the Rajputs are no longer rulers, but the people still respect their honesty and sense of justice and often come to them to settle disputes. They often fill the role of mayor in the village, and they pride themselves in being the "protectors of Hinduism." High-caste Hindus like the Rajputs pay careful attention to keeping their ethnicity pure, only arranging marriages with other Rajput clans and shunning any who go against the Hindu religion.

Pray that several families in different clans come to Christ simultaneously. In this way, Rajput believers could have the chance to demonstrate that the gospel is good news that makes them better Rajputs, instead of unnatural traitors to be cast out of the community.

If high-caste Hindus came to Christ in significant numbers, the impact on all of Indian society would be tremendous. Today, it is difficult to determine the number of believers, but it is very low. Few missionaries, Indian or foreign, serve the more than 40 million Rajputs.

❶ **Prayer Points**

- Pray that in this time of crisis and social change many Rajputs will find their identity in Christ. (1 Peter 2:9)

- The worship of lifeless idols and stars will never meet the greatest needs of high-caste Hindus. Pray that they would come to know the creator of the stars, personally. (Psalm 147:3-6)

- Pray that Rajputs in careers that put them in contact with outsiders will meet gracious Christians who will attract them to the one true God. (Philippians 2:14-15)

 Go Deeper

- Learn more about the world's 900 million Hindus. See the video and other information at *prayercast.com/hinduism* and, from the International Mission Board, *southasianpeoples.imb.org/hinduism,* which includes a downloadable prayer guide.

- Find a prayer guide for the Rajputs (and other prayer guides) at *pioneers.org/ store*

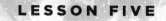
SAVIOR OF THE WORLD

Ⓜ To Memorize and Meditate On

Many Samaritans from that town believed in Him because of the woman's testimony, "He told me all that I ever did." So when the Samaritans came to Him, they asked Him to stay with them, and He stayed there two days. And many more believed because of His word. They said to the woman, "It is no longer because of what you said that we believe, for we have heard for ourselves, and we know that this is indeed the Savior of the world."

— John 4:39-42

"Nobody can force a single soul ... to turn to Christ. All that [we] ... can do, is to lift up Christ before the world, bring him into dingy corners and dark places of the earth where he is unknown, introduce him to strangers, talk about him to everyone, and live so closely with and in him that others may see that there really is such a person as Jesus."

— Betty Scott Stam, missionary martyred in China

GETTING STARTED

One of the greatest challenges Jesus faced in His earthly ministry was to break His disciples of their cultural biases. Even though the Old Testament clearly communicated God's heart for the nations and that the Messiah was also coming to be a light to the nations, most Jews were looking for a national savior who would establish His reign among the nations. The disciples were the first echelon in Jesus' strategy of taking the gospel to all nations. Yet His disciples were extremely nationalistic in their perspective of who the Messiah was and what He came to do. Through His teaching, His ministry to Gentiles, using non-Jews as spiritual object lessons, and His mandates, Jesus was intentionally and systematically reshaping their worldview.

You will be studying verses that you are familiar with. My natural tendency would be to quickly read over the verses I think I know and jot down a few thoughts. Resist that urge and take your time to discover some new insights.

❶ Whose Savior?

Read the prophetic statements about the Messiah. What will He come to do and for whom has He come?

a. Isaiah 42:5-7

[handwritten notes:]
Open eyes of blind
free Captives from prison
Release from dungeon
Fulfill Davidic Covenant

Come to Israelites (People)
Gentiles
(Everyone)

[handwritten in margin: LIGHT?]

b. Isaiah 49:6 *(Everyone)* Restore Israel, light for Gentiles
Bring salvation to ends of the earth

c. Matthew 4:12-16
Gentiles (Galilee)   Bring light to them
Open their eyes to the
Messiah

d. Luke 2:25-32
Everyone Gent + Jews   Salvation
Light for Gentiles

Jesus is the Savior of the world, not the personal possession of Israel.

❷ **Fulfilling the Scriptures**

Read Luke 4:14-30.   → Initial

a. What is the people's attitude towards Jesus' teaching? (4:14-15)

b. They handed the book of Isaiah to Jesus, but He intentionally locates the passage that He reads. To what does this prophecy, found in Isaiah 61, relate? (4:16-19)
Messiah

c. What does Jesus do after He reads the passage? What is the people's reaction to His silence? What do you think is going through their minds? (4:20)
Took mic back to his seat then finishes vs 21
+ Drops it

d. What does Jesus proclaim? (4:21)
He is the Messiah

e. How do the people respond? (4:22)
Amazed, but Skeptical

f. Why do you think Jesus made this statement? After all He had them where every preacher wants His audience, in the palm of His hand, so to speak. (4:23-27)
Skepticism of the people since they knew him
"Joseph's Son".

g. What was their response to His explanation? (4:28-29)

wanted to kill him

Jesus had just proclaimed that He was the Messiah, the One spoken of by the proph-ets, the One for whom generations of Jews had been praying. He knew that they had a nationalistic perspective of the Messiah and that they believed the Messiah was coming to be their personal deliverer. Jesus had not come to be the personal possession of Israel, He had come to be Savior of the world. He states that, "no prophet is accepted in his hometown" (Luke 4:24). It certainly seems as if they had welcomed Him. He then gives two illustrations to make His point. He uses two of their favorite prophets to reveal how God had ministered in a special way to Gentiles through them.

Jesus cut to the heart of their narrow ethnocentric perspective of the promised Mes-siah. He opened their eyes to the fact that they were not the only ones who needed a deliverer. His proclamation of release of the captives, recovery of sight to the blind, and freedom was a message of hope for the Jews and the Gentiles.

Sometimes I shake up people by saying, "Jesus is not your personal Savior." We live in a culture where personal means mine. You don't get a personal pan pizza to share it, or hire a personal trainer to share with others, and you don't want everyone using your personal computer. Now, don't get me wrong, I believe that you must receive Jesus personally and that one of the benefits of salvation is a personal and intimate relation-ship with the living God. But Jesus is not our personal possession; He is the Savior of the world.

SELAH

❸ Savior of the World

Reflect and comment on the passages below that declare the global perspective of Jesus' mission. Take your time; there is more to each of these verses than you might think.

a. John 3:16-17

b. John 6:33

c. John 8:12, 12:45-47

d. John 12:30-32

e. 1 John 4:14

❹ Disciples of the Savior

If Jesus is Savior of the world this means that you are a disciple of the Savior of the world. Begin to think through how this fact should impact your daily walk with Christ. (Example: "It means that I should integrate a global perspective in my daily prayer time.")

❺ Meditation

a. What is God teaching you through John 4:39-42?

b. Pray for the nations using the people group profile for this lesson.

"If Jesus Christ be God and died for me, then no sacrifice can be too great for me to make for Him."

— C.T. Studd, British missionary to China, India, and Africa

S E L A H

PEOPLES OF THE NORTH CAUCASUS

Russia, geographically the largest nation in the world, is home to at least 80 unique, non-Slavic people groups. Though the gospel came to the Russian people centuries ago, it has yet to penetrate many of the other groups that live within Russia's borde, and especially in the North Caucasus (KAW-kah-suhs), the most linguistically diverse region of its size on Earth.

The nine million people who call the North Caucasus home – separated from one another by nearly impassable mountains – speak more than 40 distinct and difficult-to-learn languages and hundreds of dialects. Most live in villages closed to and cut off from outsiders, strongly resist change, and are fiercely proud and protective of their cultures and Islamic traditions. No wonder mission researcher Patrick Johnstone says, "It's harder to conceive of a more difficult region to evangelize than the Caucasus."

Ministry strategists rejoice that the world's Christians show growing interest in reaching the North Caucasus, but caution that raising up prayer is more important than raising up western missionaries to enter this delicate region.

Pray for the Spirit to touch and transform more people like Shaadia (shah-ah-DEE-ah). "As a young girl, I sincerely believed Islam was indeed the religion of peace and goodness; with all my heart I searched for a close relationship with the God of Islam – like millions of honorable people in Muslim cultures around the world today. But my story is of a lack of peace in my heart."

One night she fell asleep praying to know the truth. In a dream she saw a friend who had died several years before. "She was shaking her head from side to side and repeating, 'No, Shaadia, no, it's not correct.' The dream had an intense impact, moving me to seek trust in God, not in rituals."

Shortly after the dream, she encountered a group of believers in her city and through them found what she came to understand she had sought her whole life: Jesus.

Shaadia hungrily searched the Scriptures and rejoiced when she could read the first portions in her own language. "This had a huge spiritual and emotional impact inside me that overwhelmed me. I understood spiritual truths at a much deeper level."

---

❶ **Prayer Points**

- God responds to persistent, praying people. (Luke 18:1-8) Pray that more believers around the world will open their hearts to one or more of the Caucasus people groups, committing to love and pray for them. (Philippians 1:1-7)

- Pray that the Bible would be translated into all the major languages of the Caucasus and bless them richly. (Isaiah 55:11)

- Ask the Lord of the harvest to raise up and send out workers to share the gospel, make disciples, and see healthy, effective churches planted throughout the Caucasus. (Luke 10:2)

- Pray for peace and collaboration among believers from the various language groups of the Caucasus and those from other backgrounds whom God calls to minister in this region. (Philippians 1:27)

❷ **Go Deeper**

- Download a prayer guide for all the unreached peoples of Russia from Send International at *send.org/wp-content/uploads/Unreached-People-of-Russia-Prayer-Guide-May-2013.pdf*.

- Learn more and read Shaadia's story in the March 2014 issue of The Global Prayer Digest, which is dedicated to the people of the North Caucasus. See *GlobalPrayerDigest.org*.

Video Introduction
by Jeff Lewis
pioneers.org/godsheart

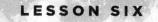

LESSON SIX

HIS CALL TO THE NATIONS

Ⓜ To Memorize and Meditate On

And Jesus came and said to them, "All authority in heaven and on earth has been given to Me. Go therefore and make disciples of all nations, baptizing them in the name of the Father and of the Son and of the Holy Spirit, teaching them to observe all that I have commanded you. And behold, I am with you always, to the end of the age." — Matthew 28:18-20

"I never made a sacrifice. Of this we ought not to talk when we remember the great sacrifice which He made who left His Father's throne on high to give Himself for us." — David Livingston, Scottish missionary to Africa

GETTING STARTED

Early in His ministry Jesus clearly communicated that He was the Messiah and that He had come to be the Savior of the world. Jesus had less than three years to liberate His Jewish disciples from their nationalistic cultural biases. It was vital for the disciples to realize that the gospel of the Kingdom is for all peoples and that His mandate was to the nations, not to a nation. Jesus uses each of these events and stories to strip away the cultural biases of His followers. This week you will continue to study how Jesus awakened His disciples to His global purpose, with deep personal implications for Christians today.

❶ Jesus and the Nations

As you study the following passages, notice what is significant about each event, what Jesus is conveying, and who His audience is.

a. Ministering to non-Jews.

　　1. Ministry to the crowds. (Matthew 4:23-25)

　　2. The faith of the Canaanite woman. (Matthew 15:21-28) Be careful how you interpret this event. In Matthew 15:1-20, Jesus had just taught on the subject of what is clean and unclean. Then notice where He took the disciples. Remember what Matthew 4:24 reveals about Jesus' ministry to Gentiles. In Matthew 15:24, to whom is Jesus speaking?

3. Jesus and the ministry in Sychar. (John 4:39-42) Notice how the villagers describe what they've discovered about Jesus after their two days together.

b. Jesus uses stories and events as object lessons for the disciples. Note that interaction with Gentiles and Samaritans and stories about them are also used by Jesus to shake up the cultural bias of the Jews.

1. The centurion's faith (Matthew 8:5-13)

2. The parable of the good Samaritan (Luke 10:30-36)

3. Jesus cleanses ten lepers (Luke 17:11-19)

c. Jesus opens the eyes of His disciples to His global purpose through His teaching.

1. Salt and light (Matthew 5:13-14)

2. Signs of the end of the age (Matthew 24:1-14)

3. The narrow door (Luke 13:22-30)

❷ Call to the Nations

After the resurrection, as Jesus moved closer to His ascension to the right hand of the Father, He made it clear that His purpose was global and His mandates were to catapult His followers to the nations. The following passages collectively comprise the "Great Commission" and restate the commission God gave to Abram found in the purpose clause of Genesis 12:3, "And in you all the families of the earth shall be blessed."

Jesus is the ultimate fulfillment of God blessing the families of the earth through Abram (Galatians 3:14). His mandate to His followers will never be understood if their only grasp of the "Great Commission" is gained from Matthew 28:19-20. Full understanding is achieved when we study all five of Jesus' restatements of the Great Commission given after the resurrection. As you study each statement notice the similar and different emphases.

a. Commissioning statements: Note how the task is defined and what the command is in each statement.

1. Matthew 28:18-20. Two hints: The imperative verb is "make disciples." "Nations" does not mean a political entity or geographical boundary of a country. "Nations" comes from the Greek word *ethne*. Identify the three verbs that help us define was is involved in discipling the nations?

2. Mark 16:15-16

3. Luke 24:44-49

4. John 20:21-23. John's account of Jesus' restatement of the commission will take on new meaning if you take the time some day to read the Gospel of John and focus on Jesus' use of the word "sent" or "send." (Examples: John 5:36-38; 6:38-39; 12:44-49.)

a. John 20:21-23 is the only commissioning statement that doesn't focus on the task, but the relationship from which the task flows. The phrase "as the Father sent me" would seem to relate to the task as it is stated in John 3:17, "…that the world might be saved through Him." The portrait of Christ which John paints is of the Word becoming flesh, accomplishing His mission through His intimate submission to the Father's will and direction.

Consider the following passages as examples of Jesus' intimate submission to the Father: John 4:34; 5:19-20; 5:30; 6:38; 10:17-18; and 14:9-11. What is Jesus communicating in these verses?

b. Notice how Jesus prays for us in John 17:17-23, especially what He requests for us from the Father and why.

5. Acts 1:3-8

Jesus not only gives us the mission of taking His message to the nations. He also empowers us to accomplish it.

b. Taking into consideration the verses you just read, write a summary statement that describes Jesus' global mandate.

---

❸ Meditation

a. What has God taught you through your meditation on Matthew 28:18-20 this week?

b. Pray for the nations using the people group profile that accompanies this lesson.

> *"Would that God would make hell so real to us that we cannot rest; heaven so real that we must have men there; Christ so real that our supreme motive and aim shall be to make the Man of Sorrows, the Man of Joy by the conversion to Him of many."*
>
> — *J. Hudson Taylor, missionary to China*

S E L A H

THE FRENCH

The largest country in Western Europe, France is home to more than 60 million people. France also welcomes more tourists than perhaps any other nation in the world. Visitors come to admire its cuisine, beautiful countryside, and impressive architecture.

Yet the materially wealthy may be spiritually poor. While the Church worldwide experiences amazing growth, Europe is the only continent where it is in severe decline. Cathedrals have become museums, congregations are closing their doors, and even in areas with deep roots of traditional Catholicism—like much of France—many are Catholic in name only. Only a small percentage of the French are practicing Catholics or affiliated with a church. They do not see Christianity in any form as an option but just a relic of the past.

Churches in a place like France struggle to survive and to adapt and respond to the ways their communities have changed. The Muslim call to prayer is heard where once church bells rang out, and when the French describe their country as Christian, they may simply mean it isn't Muslim – although now more than 10 percent of the population is.

Many of the ethnic French, if they believe in God at all, do not believe He is active in the world today. Secularism and skepticism govern most French hearts and minds. Yet spirituality is also on the rise, as expressed in growing interest in eastern religions, neo-paganism, and new-age philosophies. Psychics and spiritual healers are much in demand and have become an accepted part of mainstream society.

What would it take for more Western Europeans, be they secular, skeptical, or spiritual, to experience Christ and the message of the gospel as relevant to everyday life?

One answer may come from visitors and immigrants, which include Christians from nations that were once European colonies. Millions of them speak French, sometimes as their first language. Many come to Europe seeking a better life for themselves, but others want to "give back." African believers and others come to plant new churches and reach their neighborhoods and cities. They believe God for revival within the churches of Europe. New expressions of faith like these could make all the difference.

ⓟ Prayer Points

- Pray that more French and other Europeans will hear the gospel presented clearly and recognize its life-changing message. (2 Peter 3:9)
- Ask God to strengthen the churches of Europe by His Spirit, equipping believers to build bridges to neighbors of every background. (Acts 1:8)
- Thank God for the local Christians and evangelists and church-planters from

many lands who pray and long to see revival in Europe. (Psalm 85:6)

 Go Deeper

- Watch a Kairos video about the spiritual dynamics in Europe at *youtu.be/dEn-xAvHWRQ* and a Prayercast video about France at *prayercast.com/frane*. Find more fuel for your prayers at *imb.org/france*.

- Why not print out a map of Europe and pray over it? Memorize the names and locations of each country and intercede for them when you hear them mentioned in the news.

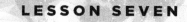

LESSON SEVEN

TO THE ENDS OF THE EARTH

M **To Memorize and Meditate On**

After this I looked, and behold, a great multitude that no one could number, from every nation, from all tribes and peoples and languages, standing before the throne and before the Lamb, clothed in white robes, with palm branches in their hands, and crying out with a loud voice, "Salvation belongs to our God who sits on the throne, and to the Lamb!"

— Revelation 7:9-10

"Obedience to God's will is the secret of spiritual knowledge and insight. It is not willingness to know, but willingness to DO God's will that brings certainty."

— Eric Liddell, Scottish gold-medal Olympian and missionary to China

GETTING STARTED

The book of Acts takes us on the journey of the Church's obedience to Jesus Christ's global mandate. It wasn't immediate obedience, however. In fact Don Richardson calls it "reluctant obedience." The disciples were hesitant to move beyond their cultural bias, but God would be proactive to thrust the Church out to accomplish His purpose voluntarily or involuntarily.

1 **The Coming of the Holy Spirit**

Read Acts 2:1-13.

a. What happened when the Holy Spirit rested on the disciples? (4, 11)

b. What was the significance of the disciples speaking languages from different regions?

c. The New Testament Church is born at Pentecost. What are the global implications at its birth?

d. See Acts 5:28 and 6:7. At this point, how are the disciples doing in fulfilling Jesus' instructions in Acts 1:8?

❷ The Ministry of the Scattered Believers

Acts 1:8 makes it clear that God empowers His church to accomplish His global mandate, but sometimes He must intervene to awaken followers when they ignore it. (Acts 8:1)

a. What mechanism does God employ to encourage the disciples to fulfill His mission mandate?

1. Among Samaritans (Acts 8:4-8; 25)

2. The Ethiopian eunuch (Acts 8:26-40)

3. Cornelius, a God-fearing Gentile (Acts 10:1-48)

4. The Hellenists (Greeks) of Antioch. (Acts 11:19-21) See also Acts 13:1-3, where we see the church in Antioch (rather than the church in Jerusalem) leading the way in sending out missionaries.

5. Notice what else God does through the church in Antioch. (Acts 1:1-3)

b. How did God persuade Peter to take the "Good News" to the Gentiles? (Acts 10:1-29)

c. How was God's purpose advanced after Peter spoke up? (Acts 10:34-48)

❸ The Jerusalem Council

The Jerusalem Council described in Acts 15:1-21 was a turning point. Read the story to discover why.

a. What was the false teaching that had entered the church? What was being added to the gospel?

b. What did Paul and Barnabas do as they traveled to Jerusalem?

c. Describe the essence of Peter's argument.

d. What was James' conclusion?

The decision made at the Jerusalem Council liberated the gospel and the church from a single cultural expression. In writing about this event, M.R. Thomas refers to the issue facing the council as the "greatest crisis" of the Church. The question facing the leaders of the Church was, "Is this new movement just another sect of Judaism, or the dynamic Church of Jesus Christ finding faithful cultural expression in all the ethne (peoples) of the earth? Take a moment and record your thought of how this question impacts the church today both locally and globally.

❹ **Hope for Both Jews and Gentiles**

a. What is Paul's understanding of his role in the mission of Christ? (Romans 15:8-21)

b. What does Revelation show us about the fulfillment of this mission? (Revelation 7:9-10)

The question of the ages is not whether God's promise to Abram will be fulfilled and disciples will be made from all nations. The Bible reveals that God's global purpose will be accomplished.

The question is, will our generation of the Church will be obedient to the mandate of Jesus Christ and participate in completing the task? And will I walk with Him, obey His mandate, and be strategically involved in His global purpose?

5 **The Church Then, the Church Now**

a. As you consider the passages you have studied from the story of the New Testament Church, what are your observations?

b. What correlations do you see between the early Church and your own local church? How can you help your church or fellowship rediscover its responsibility in Jesus' global mandate?

S E L A H

6 **Meditation**

The option of ignoring His global purpose is not granted in the Bible. He presumes obedience. The only unknowns are the details of our future involvement.

In lesson two, I opened the study with the concept of studying the Bible as one book and searching for the major themes and tracking the development of those themes throughout. During the past six lessons I have tried to guide you through the development of the theme that reveals God's global purpose and how it is connected with the theme of God blessing His people.

a. As you have worked through the study, list some of the things that you have learned and how you will apply them to your walk with Jesus.

b. Record your thoughts from your meditation on Revelation 7:9-10.

c. Pray for the nations using the people group profile associated with this lesson.

"Yes, but God had first claim on my life, and since the two conflicted, there could be no question about the result."

— Lottie Moon, American missionary China, when asked if she ever considered marriage

S E L A H

PUNJABI SIKHS

From India to Singapore, Hong Kong, Vancouver, and London, Sikhs have left their mark on society. Sophisticated, educated, and assertive, they have spread around the globe and prospered in new places without losing their cultural identity. Shopping in the great cities of India, you'll recognize Sikhs by their distinctive dress. Visiting an Indian restaurant, you may be eating Punjabi (poon-JAH-bee) food. The films of India's "Bollywood" often feature the rhythms of Punjabi music and dance.

Approximately 25 million people consider themselves Sikhs, culturally or religiously. More than 17 million live in India's Punjab state, the only place in the world where Sikhs are in the majority population. Traditionally a center of agriculture, Punjab is among the country's wealthiest regions as well as the birthplace of the Sikh faith.

Sikhism is the fifth largest of the world religions, but also the youngest. It began some 500 years ago when founder Guru Nanak (NAH-nakh) received a vision commissioning him to preach a message about the oneness of God and equality of man.

Sikhs follow the teachings of the ten Sikh *gurus* (GOO-rooz, holy teachers) whose wisdom and poetry is compiled in the holy book and final guru, *Guru Granth Sahib* (GOO-roo GRAHNTH sahb). Sikhs see the book as their religious teacher and leader. They treat it with great respect as the only tangible presence of God that they believe they will ever know. Each morning the devout gather at a *gurdwara* (good-WAH-rah, Sikh temple) to awaken the book and see what it has to say.

Sikhism emphasizes the importance of hospitality, good works, and community service. Volunteers organize feeding programs, blood drives, free medical services, and more. They are taught to share with others the good things they have received from God.

Though there are celebrated stories of Sikhs who have come to faith, there is still no movement toward Christ among them. Wonderful work to reach Sikhs outside of India is bearing some fruit, but little has been done to make disciples and plant churches among Sikhs in India.

One Punjabi Christian said, "my dream is for a church to be planted among Sikhs where they can draw on all the wonderful things about their culture – their assertiveness, their hospitality, their progressiveness – and worship God in a way unique to them."

ⓟ Prayer Points

- Pray that Sikhs' respect for scripture would create an openness to read the Bible and know the living Word. (John 1:1)

- Many Sikhs have worked hard to build wealth and successful businesses; they have few felt needs. Ask God to create in Sikhs a hunger and awareness of their need for Him. (John 6:44)

- Pray for Sikhs who have immigrated to the U.S., Canada, England, and Australia. May local believers in these places befriend them and introduce them to Jesus. (Acts 17:26-27)

ⓖ Go Deeper

Look for Sikhs where you live or when you travel. Learn about Sikhism from a Sikh point of view at *sikhs.org*. Find many resources to help you understand Sikhs and learn how to recognize and reach out to them at *southasianpeoples.imb.org/Sikhism*.

Read Authors statement "One of the blessing...
*The 1st lesson we discovered that God
does all things for His Name, Renown + Glory
- THIS IS HIS MISSION

- Call back to lesson 3   Psalm 46:10   mood & verb
    Ivitation? – Command/Order (Imperitive)
    Declaration – Process
- Consider importance + priority of the Command
    ⚹ Jeremiah 9:23-24
            back to end of Chp 7 –
        Prophsyg in Judah when its all going
        bad discussing sin + punishment
            VS 24 is Key + through end of chp.
        "I am the LORD" Ex 6:2-8
            God's promise of deliverance + Redemption
                (back to lesson 2 Joseph)
        Understan + Knows 9:24
            ⚹ Phil 3:7-10
        Calling us to Intimacy, to KNOW Him
- Mobilization Defined.
    - Table discussion
    - Brief Spiritual Disciplines . John Piper –
                                        "what is the purpose
    ⚹ Joel + Hurston Team ⚹   of Missions"

LESSON EIGHT

PERSONAL APPLICATION

Ⓜ To Memorize and Meditate On

"But you are a chosen race, a royal priesthood, a holy nation, a people for His own possession, that you may proclaim the excellencies of Him who called you out of darkness into His marvelous light."

— 1 Peter 2:9

"All my friends are but One, but He is all sufficient."

— William Carey, British missionary to India

GETTING STARTED

Every disciple of the Savior of the world should be committed to the process of developing a lifestyle that reflects and daily participates in the mission of God. One of the blessings of our salvation is that we have been liberated from the slavery of living for self so that we might live engaged in His mission (2 Corinthians 5:15). Our natural inclination is to develop an egocentric and ethnocentric faith. It is essential that every follower of Christ globally develop themselves biblically, spiritually, and practically in relation to the mission of God.

❶ Intimacy and Mobilization

Conventional wisdom says the way you mobilize people toward missions is to get them on a mission trip. If that is the foundational motivation for missions, it may suggest that our primary motive is man's need, and that we are persuaded to be involved through experiences. Notice, though, how God's mission relates to His call to intimacy.

a. Go back to Psalm 46:10. What is God's invitation? How do you think the invitation is related to the declaration?

Lesson 3

b. Consider the profound nature, privilege, and priority of the invitation as it is reflected in these passages, as well.

1. Jeremiah 9:23-24

53

2. Hosea 6:6

3. John 17:3, 20-23

4. Philippians 3:7-11

c. Notice how emphatically God repeats the declaration of Psalm 46:10 in these passages.

1. Psalm 22:27-28

2. Habakkuk 2:14

3. Malachi 1:11, 14

A biblically based pursuit of knowing God will result in a life committed to His mission. As you passionately pursue the knowledge of God, He will infuse His heart, purpose, perspective, and mission into your life.

In the first lesson of this study you discovered that God does all things for His name, renown, and glory. This is His mission. He is the one who motivates, directs, and empowers His people to accomplish His mission. Ask the Father to imprint on your heart a passion for Him that matches the passion He has for His name. When this passion becomes the driving force in your life, then mission trip experiences and information about the needs of the nation can lead you to make wise decisions, not decisions based in guilt or momentary excitement.

Take a moment to consider what the Father is saying to you through His Word.

SELAH

❷ Mobilization Defined

To mobilize may be defined as "to assemble or marshal into readiness for active service." In the missions community, the term is often confused with missions recruitment. If you are not going someplace, you can always be a sender, pray-er, welcomer, etc. But our readiness for active service is not about selecting a title or role in the missions subculture created by the Church. Rather, our "readiness for active service" is demonstrated by a biblical lifestyle transformation. We have been liberated from the slavery of living for ourselves. We are mobilized when Christ is the passion of our lives and the cause of Christ guides our life decisions.

How might the following verses related to this kind of mobilization?

a. 2 Corinthians 5:17

Psalm 1?

b. Romans 12:1-2

c. Galatians 2:20

❸ Spiritual Disciplines

Mobilization flows from who we are in Christ. Spiritual disciplines are the spiritual exercises we do in order to walk by faith in the reality of our new life in Christ. One of the first steps in developing a global context of this new life in Christ is to integrate a global perspective in these spiritual disciplines. Take time to consider and record how you will begin to practically integrate these concepts into your daily walk with Christ.

a. Discipline of awareness

1. Biblical awareness

Through this study you have either started or continued the process of developing a biblical understanding of God's global purpose. This process should be a life-long journey of biblical discovery, not a one-time event. As you read the Bible, ask the Holy Spirit to continue to sensitize you to His global purpose.

2. Historical awareness

Read Hebrews 11:32-12:3. The great cloud of witnesses is not limited to Old Testament characters, but includes those who in the last two thousand years have been faithful to the global mandate of Christ. They have manifested the power of his resurrection and participated in the fellowship of His suffering. We can learn much from their lives. Consider how you can develop an historical awareness of the last 2000 years of God's activity of accomplishing His global mission.

3. Contemporary awareness

We live in a day and age where the visible activity of God is greater than any other time in the history of man. The problem is that most Christians don't know what's going on. Consider how you can begin to connect with the "stealth" activity of the kingdom around the world. Discover what God is doing around the world.

b. Discipline of intercession

1. Interceding for the front-line workers

Read Romans 15:30-31, Ephesians 6:19-20, Colossians 4:2-4, 1 Thessalonians 5:25, and 2 Thessalonians 3:1-2. If Paul needed the prayer of the saints, what do you think about our missionaries? Make note of the specific things that Paul asked them to pray about. This is not a bad place to start in our prayers for those on the front-lines, instead of a blanket request like "be with our missionaries today and bless them."

2. Interceding for our brothers and sisters in Christ around the world

Read Ephesians 6:18. You will one day be worshipping with them before the throne of God and the Lamb. Are you praying for them? Are you praying specifically for the followers of Jesus Christ in specific areas of the world where witnessing for Christ is an issue of great consequence, many times resulting in death?

3. Interceding for the unreached

Read Ezekiel 22:30 and 1 Timothy 2:1-4. There are thousands of people groups, totaling more than 2.9 billion people, who have not heard the gospel. Are you praying regularly and specifically for any of them?

4. Interceding for local and global events

Read Nehemiah 1:1-4. What promoted Nehemiah's prayer and fasting? What would be the possible avenues today that would relate to what prompted Nehemiah to fast and pray and that could lead you to do the same? As you listen, read, or watch, ask the Holy Spirit to guide you in how to respond to the things that are brought to your attention.

c. Discipline of choice

As a steward of God's possessions, how do the choices you make reflect God's global purpose? Consider how the truth of each of the following Bible passages would relate to the broader biblical context of God's global purpose.

1. Money (Matthew 6:19-24; Luke 16:1-13)

2. Time (Psalm 90:12)

3. Relationships (2 Corinthians 6:14)

4. Lifestyle (Matthew 6:25-34)

5. Location (Mark 16:15, Hebrews 11:8-10)

d. Discipline of obedience

Read John 14:15, 21, 23-24, 31; 15:9-10, 14. Reflect on these verses in the context of Jesus' global mandate.

e. Discipline of worship

Read Psalm 96. Does your worship reflect the praise of your tribal deity or the God of all nations? When you read through the Psalms, notice how intentional the psalmist is in declaring that God is not just the God of Israel but the God of all creation.

f. Discipline of fasting

Read Isaiah 58:3-12. Jesus never commanded us to fast; He assumed that we would fast (Matthew 6:16, "whenever you fast …"). Does your fasting connect with God's global purpose? To what should our fasting lead us?

g. Discipline of fellowship

Read Hebrews 10:24-25. How do these truths relate to God's global purpose and our responsibility in the local church?

h. Discipline of involvement

Read Matthew 25:31-46. Take your time in writing your thoughts in the context of what you have studied the last eight lessons.

i. Discipline of cross-cultural evangelism

Read Acts 1:8. Sharing your faith cross-culturally is not just for a select few; it is the responsibility of all who receive the Holy Spirit.

---

❹ **Meditation**

Feeling overwhelmed? I have thrown a lot of stuff at you in this lesson. Please do not try to do everything that you have studied. If you do you will get tired quickly and probably quit. As you pray through what you have just studied, select one or two disciplines and receive from God the grace to be faithful in those, then add another discipline, and so on. Develop faithfulness in the process. This is a life-long journey.

a. Record what you think the Lord might be guiding you to focus on next.

b. What has God been teaching you through your meditation of 1 Peter 2:9?

> "The trouble with nearly everybody who prays is that he says 'Amen' and runs away before God has a chance to reply. Listening to God is far more important than giving Him your ideas."
> — Frank Laubach, American missionary to the Philippines, mystic, and champion of literacy

SELAH

NOTES

NOTES

RESOURCES

BOOKS

- *The Mission of God,* Christopher J.H. Wright
- *The Mission of God's People,* Christopher J.H. Wright
- *Discovering the Mission of God,* Mike Barnett, editor
- *Invitation to World Missions,* Timothy C. Tennent
- *Salvation to the Ends of the Earth,* Andreas J. Kostenberger and Peter T. O'Brien
- *Transforming Mission,* David J. Bosch
- *Let the Nations Be Glad!* John Piper
- *A Holy Ambition,* John Piper
- *Perspectives on the World Christian Movement: A Reader, Fourth Edition,* Ralph E. Winter and Steve C. Hawthorne, editors
- *Tentmaking,* Patrick Lai
- *The Open Secret,* Lesslie Newbigin
- *Western Christians in Global Mission: What's the Role of the North American Church?* Paul Borthwick
- *Preach and Heal,* A Biblical Model for Missions, Charles Fielding
- *A Wind in the House of Islam,* David Garrison
- *Operation World,* Jason Mandryk
- *From Jerusalem to Irian Jaya,* Ruth A. Tucker

If you are only going to read one book I would recommend *Let the Nations Be Glad.* The second book would be *The Mission of God.*

PERIODICALS AND NEWS

- *Evangelical Missions Quarterly*—thoughtful articles on mission issues, *emqonline.org.*
- *Mission Frontiers*—a bulletin of the U.S. Center for World Mission, *missionfrontiers.org.*
- *Global Prayer Digest*—highlighting unreached peoples, *globalprayerdigest.org.*
- *Missions Catalyst*—weekly digest of mission news and resources, *missionscatalyst.org.*

- The Traveling Team—challenging students to reach the nations, *thetraveling-team.org.*
- Joshua Project—with profiles and data about unreached peoples, *joshuaproject.net.*
- Mission Next—a gateway to opportunities in mission, *missionnext.org.*
- Go Corps—go for two years, *gocorps.org.*
- Pioneers—church planting among the unreached, *pioneers.org.*
- International Mission Board—connecting churches with unreached peoples, *imb.org.*

CPSIA information can be obtained
at www.ICGtesting.com
Printed in the USA
BVOW08s1343040418
512448BV00011B/916/P